My Life with KOOL JOE

KOOL JOE & KITTEN

A True Love Story -Transformation *of* Diamonds in the Rough

Written by

Dr. Lynette T. Smith

Balboa Press books may be ordered through booksellers or by contacting:

Balboa Press
A Division of Hay House
1663 Liberty Drive
Bloomington, IN 47403
www.balboapress.com
1 (877) 407-4847

Because of the dynamic nature of the Internet, any web addresses or links contained in this book may have changed since publication and may no longer be valid. The views expressed in this work are solely those of the author and do not necessarily reflect the views of the publisher, and the publisher hereby disclaims any responsibility for them.

Any people depicted in stock imagery provided by Thinkstock are models, and such images are being used for illustrative purposes only.
Certain stock imagery © Thinkstock.

ISBN: 978-1-5043-5380-9 (sc)
ISBN: 978-1-5043-5381-6 (e)

Print information available on the last page.

Balboa Press rev. date: 06/02/2016

BALBOA
PRESS
A DIVISION OF HAY HOUSE

This book is dedicated to the memory of my husband Joseph Wilfred Smith (November 5, 1942 - December 4, 2015). Joseph was a husband, father, grandfather and an extraordinary band director and instrumental music teacher.

Some of his students called him Poppa Smith, Grandpa and the Maestro. His children called him Daddy, Dad and Pops. I called him KOOL JOE and JW.

May your spirit of individuality, and artistry continue to live on as you have now

become a part of the Great Cloud of Witness.

Foreword

Writing this story is my therapy. When I'm feeling overwhelmed from the loss of Joseph, I find solace in writing my experiences with him. I affectionately called him JW AKA Kool Joe.

These journey experiences were also written for my children and grandchildren. It is hoped that they will see their parents and grandparents in a more human light. I want them to know that we were not perfect. We were just two imperfect human beings struggling to be better even though situations in our childhood and adulthood might have given them another perspective. I pray that they will see that their parents never quit in believing that life could be better and that "winners never quit and quitters never win"

Lastly, just maybe, our marriage journey will help and encourage some married couple who are going through turbulent and trying times will learn some of the lessons that we learned on our journey together, and that each couple will make the decision not to quit but to strive hard to learn how to forgive and love each other on this earthly journey. It is hoped that they will continue to love and support one another. This story is about two people on a roller coaster ride from youth to maturity which eventually ended in a peaceful destination. In other words, this story is about two people fighting personal wars within themselves and deciding in the end that working together was the way each of them could allow God to produce the diamond that was in each of them. I do not regret all the moments I spent with this renaissance man. I would do it all over again if I could do it again with him.

KOOL JOE & KITTEN

Contents

Now let the story begin

His family and classmates called him Wilfred, His school mates called him Wilfred and Rat Man. His college classmates called him Joe and Rice Man because he loved rice. His Children called him dad and Pops. I called him JW and KOOL Joe. He called himself the Mellow Fellow but if you asked his full name he would say "My name is Joseph" Joseph means he shall add and he did:

He added:

Ronald Tyrone

Leonard Spencer

Curtis Elliott

Tyfanni Nekeisha

And because they were apart of him they did add:

Ronald Tyrone, II

TABIA Mariah

Tykiah Nimah

Jamel Alexander

Jori Aliyah

Jarren Andrew

Tierah Alexis

Tamia LeShay

Jai Syncere

Tyee Shabazz

And in the future they will add

and Joseph will live on.

He affectionately called me Kitten because I was soft. quiet and needed protection.

The Children call me Ma, Mom and Mommy. Family call me Nette, and Penny. Friends called me twenty-five cents and Squirt. Some acquaintances called me Red because I use to wear my hair red. Colleagues called me Mrs. Smith, Smith, mother, Dr mom and Overseer. I call myself Lynette Ruth because I'm named by my daddy, Curtis Preston Townsend, a Pentecostal minister, and my name means beautiful. I attracted KOOL Joe and he couldn't let go until death came and took him but the love still goes on.

Sayings of KOOL JOE:

"How far can you go into the woods? Only halfway then you're coming out."

"Listen to the question before you answer."

"I'm a teacher. I can teach a person anything if he just pays attention."

"There is no one like you. Look at the palm of your hand. You are unique. You're one of a kind.

There will be no one like you before you or after you!"

"There is no ball playing in heaven but music is up there."

"I can't sing but I know when it sounds right."

"Logistics boy. You hold people accountable by using logistics!"

"God gave me the gift of teaching and I'm going to give it away to anyone who wants to learn.

I'm going back to God empty."

"Just be you."

"A gone is gone. It does not matter who left. You or me. It's still a gone."

"Good sense will make cents."

"Don't turn to the right or left, if you want to get to heaven, you've got to go straight."

"You can't recycle wasted time",

"A hard thing about business is minding your own business".

"Children need more models than critics".

"Jumping to conclusion is bad exercise".

"Patience is counting down before blasting off"

"God's last name is not dammit",

Chapter One — How I Met Joseph

Here I am 73 years old, on December 4, 2015, I lost the love of my life just six months away from fifty years of being married to him. I feel like a school girl who has lost her first love.

It was a cold and chilly 32 degrees' day, November 29, 1942, a baby girl was born to Curtis P. and Ruth Anderson Townsend in Russeville, (Camp Quarters, South Carolina. Her father named her Lynette Ruth.

I had a normal childhood. I grew up in a community of people who came from different country towns to Russellville, (Camp") to better themselves economically. My father served as the minister of a Holiness church in that community. My father also pastored a church in North Carolina. My parents married when my mother was seventeen and he was twenty-seven years old. My dad promised my mother that if she would marry him, he would see that she finished high school and college. With that agreement they were married.

My mother stayed home with me until age five. At age five she went back to high school with me in tow. I had the pleasure of staying with the first grade teacher for two years. My mother graduated and her plan was to enter college in North Carolina. On one of his pastoral trips, our home was destroyed by fire. As a result, we went to live with my mother's parents in Cross, SC. I then became my grandmother's baby. She called me Penny because I was so tiny. My mother entered college at Fayetteville State College now called Fayetteville State University and I entered the second grade at Zion School in Cross. My mother graduated from college when I was in the sixth grade. After graduation she began working as a teacher immediately in Berkeley County SC. Around 1954-55, a new school for African American students was built in Cross and all black schools in that area consolidated. The new school was named Central School. It housed elementary through high school students. My mother was employed there as a sixth grade teacher. My mother eventually became principal of that elementary school.

On November 5, 1942 while the Spanish explorers discovered corn in Cuba, a baby boy was born to Ronald David and Elizabeth (Peggy) Smith. He was a building contractor and she was a registered nurse. They named their son, Joseph Wilfred. Joseph's early childhood was what we would consider to be a normal childhood growing up in Charleston, South Carolina. He went to school and enjoyed fishing and crabbing with his dad. At the age of eight his mother became ill and passed away. Joseph and his brother moved to Ridgeville, South Carolina to be reared by his aunt and uncle, John and Myrtle Duberry. I met Joseph when we were thirteen years old. We were eight graders at Central Elementary School, Cross, SC. He was dark complexioned very slim, he always had a sullen look on his face. He always wore a short suit jacket and kept a pencil behind his ear.

I in turn was also petite, light complexioned and very introverted. Even though he did not appear to be friendly he had the knack of making friends easily. I later learned that Joseph was my Cyreno. The love letters I received from one of our classmates during elementary school was written by Joseph. Joseph was one of the first student to joined the newly formed band at school. His instrument of choice was the trumpet. Little did we know that we were destined to be together.

Elementary School

In ninth grade my parents moved to a town called Moncks Corner, SC. Joseph and I did not meet again until 1960. I was enrolled as a freshmen at Berkeley Training High School. In 1960 our school was hosting the Honor Society Program for all the district African American high schools in our district. My task was to give the welcome address on the program and guess who gave the response to the welcome? You got it right, Joseph. Now he is tall, still thin, his sullen look has disappeared and he had a little smile. He is still dark but now he is handsome. We spoke, he smiled. No clue, I had my circle of friends and he had his. Just another guy I met again. In 1960 we graduated from high school and entered college. He entered Claflin College and I entered South Carolina State College, both colleges were located in Orangeburg, South Carolina. The colleges were located next to each other. It was hoped that Joseph would become a preacher by attending Claflin instead he chose music as his major and I chose Business Administration.

Chapter Two — College Life

One day who do I meet again in college, no longer called Wilfred or Rat Man, but now he is called Joseph, Rice Man. He is still tall, dark, handsome, no longer sullen looking and he has developed the use of using words. We called it "rap". Later he told me that he learned words and their usage by studying the dictionary at night after working in the fields. Needless to say, he caught my attention. We became friends. He would call on me frequently at the dormitory. The dorm monitor would say "Lynette Townsend you have a caller." Thank you". I would rush downstairs and there he was. Always soft spoken, always, sweet and mannerly. He would grab my hand and we would just walk the campus and finally stop under what we called our tree and kiss. Still I had my friends and he had his.

Both of us in our sophomore year joined a fraternity and sorority. He became a member of Alpha Phi Alpha Fraternity(Alpha) and I became a member of Alpha Kappa Alpha Sorority (AKA). My mother was responsible for me joining a sorority because she felt that if I joined other young ladies I might lose my inability to connect with others since I was an only child. As a young child I did not make friends easily. My mother saw that would be a limitation to my getting ahead in the world. Joseph loved being an Alpha Man. He would always say "we are servants of all, we transcend all," Yet he still had his friends and I had mine.

The Civil Rights Movement

Like the poet, Charles Dickens said" It was the best of times, it was the worst of times".

Inside the gates of our campuses we as students felt safe from the dangerous elements of segregation. A new message, however, was being brought on our campus: We were told that we were not equal in the eyes of society and the law. What's new about that most of us thought. Tell us something we do not know we demanded. And they did. Civil rights leaders told us that our task was to war against those who oppressed us. Our role would be that of "demonstrators". "If you want your freedom, you must sacrifice and our first assignment was to learn how to be a demonstrator. Rallies were held at Trinity United Methodist Church right across the street from the campuses. Both of us joined the cause for our freedom. Our professors taught that it was our duty as students to participate in the struggle. They explained that demonstrating was dangerous and we could end up in jail or worse, we could be killed. I don't know whether it was the thrill of the moment or did we really think about the danger or did we really believe we could make a difference. Whatever the reason, we enlisted. Demonstrations for us landed both of us in jail. Joseph was sent to one of the newly built correctional centers and I was taken to the Orangeburg City Jail. In the jail cells there were four girls to cell. Inside the cell was a commode which did not work for the entire time we were there. I remembered the food was terrible. One meal was grits and syrup. We were told not to throw it in the trash. We were told if we threw it in the trash, they jailer would not allow them to bring us food. The leaders of the movement persuaded our parents not to bail us out of jail. We stayed in jail a week. That's how long it took the movement to raise our bail. Many of our classmates could not located. However, after a period of time, we were located and freed.

However, by our junior year, our relationship seemed to cool. At that time my life appeared to shift away from him. On my way to Botany class one day I met this six foot nine-inch basketball player. We are in the same class. It wasn't long before we fell for each other. He was from Philadelphia, Pennsylvania. He called me Squirt and I called him Dee. It looked like it was going to be a smooth ride. The next year, Dee dropped out of college, however, our relationship still continued.

Kitten in college

Chapter Three — New York Venture

In 1964, I graduated as a Business Administration major. Joseph graduated as a music major. He went his way; I went to the Big Apple, New York City. Life was on a roll. I was finally free from the restriction and rules of my parents. Dee and I resumed our relationship. He was a policeman in Philadelphia and I was a typesetter. Life was on a high and all was right with the world. Then trouble began. Physically, I was a wreck and could not work. I began bleeding and no matter how many doctors my aunt took me to the bleeding would not stop. Finally, the diagnosis came: I am pregnant. Dee got scared and ran away because he was hiding something he should have told me when we met. He took the coward way out and stop visiting. My parent came and took me home. I went home in disgrace. As I reflect on this part of the journey, it was strange that I was never introduced to his family or had any connections with his friends.

But, all was not lost! Then one day a friend took me for a ride. For the life of me I don't know how we ended up at the bus station and who do we meet there? No one but Joseph Wilfred Smith. What made me get out of the car and go to his car? Why would you get out of the car and you are six months pregnant? After forty-nine years I am still trying to figure that out.

We met again. You would think this fellow would act surprised at my condition. He acted as if he did not notice. From that day, he called me every night and talked to encourage me. Then to top it off he came and asked my father's permission to take me on a date. What kind of guy does that? What kind of guy wants to be seen with someone carrying someone else baby? Crazy you say? In retrospect, I say he was a man destined!

During my pregnancy I suffered from anemia and had to be taken to the doctor each week to receive a shot. I slowly recovered. On June 23, 1965 I gave birth to a bouncing baby girl. I named her Gwendolyn Yvonne, after my best girlfriend who I had known since the age of fourteen. Joseph was happy as if the baby was his. Then the calls and the visits stopped. I tried getting in touch with Dee by writing to him. He responded by writing my parents and he told them even though he loved me he could not get married to me. He did not tell them why but when I sent him a picture by my girlfriend he confessed to her that he could not marry me because he was already married. He was married before he came to college and was the father of two boys. I never heard from him again. Later years I found out that Dee died when he was in his thirties.

Lessons Learned: Never give yourself to another person without thinking it through. If you make the decision to continue and you give yourself to that person without protecting yourself, you cannot control the results of the situation.

Meet his family and try to find out about his or her background.

Chapter Four — Meeting Joseph Again

I searched for a job after I had the baby and it seemed as it was not to be. Community and rural culture made it almost impossible. The culture looked down on a young lady that had a baby if she was not married. The culture hypocritically, enforced that and as a single mother you were an outcast. However, my mother's principal knew of a job opening in another county, so he called the principal and got me an interview. The principal came to my home and interviewed me for the job as a Typing teacher. Before the principal arrived, my mother took my baby for a ride so that it looked like I was just a single woman looking for a job. My mother was always my advocate. That principal hired me as Typing teacher at Jenkins Hill School, Harleyville, SC. My parents said to me before I left home again" Here is your chance to get your life back, you can go where you want to, and be what you need to be, the baby stays with us". Later on my parents adopted Gwendolyn as their daughter. However, she always knew that I was her mother. So, for a second time, I left the security of my parents' home.

At the first faculty meeting, the principal introduced the new teachers and guess who is on the faculty as band director? You guessed it: Joseph W Smith. Still tall, dark and handsome and still smiling and still rapping. He looked at the other male teachers and said to them to leave me alone because I was his. Immediately we became friends again. As time went on I became his girl and we fell in love with each other even though he was engaged to someone else. We went and did everything together which was not a lot because at the time he did not have come a car. After school he would come by and I would cook to show off my skills as a cook. After eating he would stay and he would leave around ten at night. He would walk to where he stayed which was approximately two miles away. This took courage on his part because during that time it was dangerous for a black man to be out walking alone at that time of night. But he would do it each day and then it would start over again. Friends who had cars would invite us over. The relationship still continued. Then he got a car. If I remember correctly it was a white Ford.

Joseph introduced me to so many things during the inception of our relationship. For instance, he schooled me on how to dress going on a date and your final destination for the night is a hotel. He would say" put on your finest outfit, carry your best bag and walk with your head high through the front door with me." We did and registered for the night. You would think I learned my lesson from the first relationship? I did not. You see, Joseph had a way that he could convince you that if he said a rooster could fly, you did not argue, you just did what it took to hook that rooster up. From that one experience we never did back seat lovemaking again. It was always first class.

Later he purchased his first car a black 1965 Thunderbird. The front passenger seat was mine. No other young lady was allowed to ride in the front passenger side not while I was in the car. Then another time he influenced me to go on a trip with him. It was the final day of school for the Christmas holiday Joseph was taking me home. Just as we are about half way to my home, he said "Let's go to New York! Me: I can't my mother is expecting me home." After all I had a baby at home.

He: Aren't you head of the Yearbook staff?

Me: yes

He: Call your mother and tell her you have some work to complete on the yearbook and you'll be home at the end of the week.

Me: (dialing: mom,)" I have some work to do on the yearbook. Will be home later."

Mom: okay.

Off we went, stopped in Columbia, picked up his cousin. Next stop; New York City. We stayed in the finest hotel, we had a ball, but, On our way back home .... And as usual, trouble struck again. We are laughing thinking we have pulled off the biggest treachery, a car came out of nowhere and hits us. His car was damaged and needed to be repaired. But I needed to get home. This shy, unassuming guy became courageous again and called my parents to inform them that we were in New York and that we had an accident. He reassured my parents that we were alright. Immediately my mother responded, you're not married are you? He: Oh no ma'am. My mother never explained why she asked that question. He then bought tickets for us and we headed back to South Carolina.

At that time when you traveled on the train you could pull the cord to notify the conductor that you were at your destination. When we are near my destination, Joseph pulled the cord, the train slowed to a stop and I refused to get off. I was afraid of what my parents would say so to calm me he allowed the train to pull off and we headed for the next destination which was Charleston. Mind you, he does not have a car to get me back to Moncks Corner, but this guy does not panic. He reassured me that everything was going to be alright. After all, we were together. Lucky for us we met someone from Moncks Corner at the station and he agreed to take us to my parent's home. My father thanked him for bringing me home safely and asked how could he help him. Joseph said," Just a ride back to the train station sir so I can go back to New York and get my car." He went back to New York. You would think after this episode this young man would have said " this is a crazy girl! I'm getting out of this relationship. But he never did.

When I think in retrospect, this guy knew the good, bad, and the ugly about my life and I really knew nothing about his. In fact, because he looked good, protected me, and we always had a good time, I did not ask or care about his life or why he lived with his aunt and uncle. Eventually he told me his mother died and he and his younger brother came to live with them. I didn't realize he too was struggling and battling his demons of abandonment, fear and distrust and I was also fighting my demon.

Because I was an only child I was always afraid that those I loved would leave me and I would be left alone. Later in our relationship he trusted me enough to tell me about his father. He would talk about his dad with a gleam in his eyes. He would talk about as a child they went crabbing and other fun things they did together. His highlight was about His days at the Catholic school in Charleston. He shared about his riding to school in a cab but one day he missed it and he walked home. After that They bought him a raincoat and a bicycle and he rode his bicycle to school. But he could never say that his father really abandoned him and his brother. He had no problem telling me that his mom, who was a registered nurse became sick and eventually died. But he could never articulate that they were abandoned by their father. He was eight and his brother was two. They moved to live with his aunt, who was his mother's sister. His father visited occasionally. His vivid memory was of his father buying them a train and promised to return. He never did. His uncle would take them to visit his dad but each time they went, a lady would come on the porch and say he was not home but his truck was always there. Eventually his uncle said we will not go back again. He often stated he was alright because he knew the aunt and uncle would take good care of his brother.

Lesson Learned: Take the time to know your prospective mate's family, his thoughts and his goals. Talk to older relatives about the family and your prospective mate's struggles. You might learn something.

Well back to us!!!

Kool Joe & Kitten—In the Beginning

Chapter Five — Married Life

After the Christmas holiday was over, we went back to work and as usual our relationship continued. We went everywhere together. I noticed that he drank but since it did not affect our relationship I began to abet him in his drinking by buying him alcohol and a case to put the alcohol in so that he could hide it from others. Also when we went to night clubs, I willingly participated in the talent competition to win him a fifth of liquor. On the nights they had singing competition, he would say to me " Go up baby and sing and win me the liquor" You're good you can do it and I did and won. I did not realize I was setting a precedence that I would regret for the rest of my life. I never developed the habit of drinking because I did not like the way it made me feel or acted. I vowed that I would never drink alcohol because I wanted to be in control. Whatever happened it would be my decision and not the alcohol. Trouble started again.

I got pregnant again. I refused to go home. Joseph again stepped in and showed courage. He rented a house in St. George SC and we began to set up housekeeping. He did not propose but it just seemed to be understood by both of us that the alternative was marriage. We went to the court house filled the application to be married. After two weeks of living together, it appeared as if he was not going to pick up the license up for us to get married. I told him to make up his mind. He went to the court house and picked up the license and stopped by the jeweler for a ring. The ring cost ten dollars. Later that day he went out for a little while, came back later from picking up his younger brother and my girlfriend and said to me "Get dress". The only dressy dress I had was a black dress with a white front. I dressed in it and he got dressed in his suit and shoes with no socks. The preacher came, we got married, June 4, 1966. After that we went to bed and went to sleep. He had taken care of the situation again. I did not have to worry or go home in shame. That's it. No crowd! No reception, no honeymoon but I am married now! The next day we went to tell our parents. In the beginning of our relationship we loved and enjoyed being with each other. I found out later on that would be the key to our lasting relationship. This marriage did not set too well with our families. Eventually my parents came around and gave us a reception. But, his aunt did not accept me at first. It took time for me to prove that I was worthy of her nephew. She had other plans for him. She had sent him to college with the hopes that he would become a preacher. She was getting use to him being a band director but this was asking too much. Later she accepted me when we brought the baby to her. We later became the best of friends and my love for her grew. She became my best friend.

One thing I have learned is that you only get to know someone by living with them and establishing a relationship not just with him or her but with the entire family. They became my family and not just my in laws. Our marriage began with all fun and games. I enjoyed being the center of attention. But living with someone who was pregnant is another story. And I am sure Joseph wasn't prepared for my mood swings and my cravings. Sometimes at ten o'clock at night I wanted fried shrimps. He would get out of bed and drive to the next town and bring me shrimps. Now the next town was approximate 30 miles away. Whatever I wanted he tried get for me to make me happy.

Then things began to change. I had to give up my job because custom dictated that a pregnant woman whether single or married if you were pregnant it was expected that you would resign your position. You were not to be in school working with children and pregnant. So I did. Each day I would wait for him to return from work. And each day when he returned from work, when he got home he would walk by me and would not speak. He would go in our back bedroom and stay for about thirty minutes, then he would come out and speak to me. This I could not accept. Where did this moody person come from? How dare he act like he did not see me. Slowly, however, we got to know each other. I finally realize that he needed time to unwind from the day. But, this he could not articulate.

The first time he stayed out all night and I had to stay alone, I was terrified. Imagine I'm in a strange place, pregnant and alone. To make matters worse it is close to my birthday. The evening of my birthday he returned and said to me "get dress we're going out." When I asked him where he was his answer was listen a gone is a gone, when you go, you are gone. I miss you. A gone is a gone but I'm here now. I got dressed and he took me to a hotel where he and some of his gave me a surprise birthday party. That night we spent the night at the hotel. That was his way of saying I'm sorry. Call me crazy, I was just glad that he was back. I needed him and he needed me. But I began to think of of ways to retaliate and make him pay for leaving me alone.

One day he is showed me how to shoot a BB gun and I saw my chance to retaliate and I did. He told me I could not be trusted with any kind of gun and from then on he never showed me how to shoot any weapons again because he said he had married a crazy woman. Whenever he was pleased with me he called me Kitten but if I ever heard him called me Woman I knew I had gone too far. On the weekends however, he always invited his friends over and we would have a party. We would cook and it would always end up into drinking. I learned a valuable lesson during these parties and that was I was not to make the mistake that his friends were my friends. In fact, he would become very angry if I held a conversation with one of his friends or if I would engage in the conversation while he was talking. After they left he would let me know under no circumstances I must consider them to be my friends. He would say they are men, I don't trust them around you and never engage in the conversation while I am talking to them. I had to understand that the conversation was personal and it was not one for me to be a part of the entertainment. I learned early on he was jealous. I also learned that when he was with me the real journey was to experience and always enjoy him while he was with me.

Our marriage continued to be a little rocky but each crisis we would experience he would come through. Nevertheless, I became frustrated and decided that my baby would not be born in this situation. So, I asked him to take me to visit my parents. While I'm there, the baby was born. January 28, 1967, a beautiful baby boy. His father was not there. He later called to see how I was doing and if I was ready to come home. It was then he found out that I had given birth and he had a son. That afternoon he showed up at the hospital. He was proud and informed me that the baby's name would be Ronald Tyrone. Instead of naming him after himself he chose to name his first son after his baby brother, Ronald David. He reasoned in his mind when his brother was sick when he was younger that if anything happened to his brother he would always have Ronald with him. He loved his brother to a fault. He never allowed me or anyone else to speak ill about his brother. After three days, I was discharged from the hospital and he came and took me to our home in St George. He was happy and proud.

But the actual responsibility of providing for his new family was a challenge for him. He had so many decisions to make such as do I party or do I see if my wife and child have heat and food. After while all of those indecisions made our relationship strained plus to make matters worse he did not renew his contract as band director.

Lessons Learned: Never force marriage upon someone just because you are pregnant. Make sure that both of you are making a marriage covenant because you love and care for one another.

Always be quick to forgive. Do not hold un forgiveness in your heart. You are an imperfect too.

Let the marriage proposal be his idea. If he chooses to walk away, let him and you move forward.

Take time to learn your partner's ways. Remember the two of you were not reared alike.

We decided that if our relationship was going to survive, we would move to my hometown. My father found us a house. The house was located next door to my parents. Imagine moving next door to your wife's parents where the father is a minister and the mother is a principal. Joseph began to feel like a fish out of water. I was pleased because anytime I wanted to go home I could and if I had a problem all I had to do was go next door to my parents. My dad never took sides, however, my mother was a different story. During this time, I began to find out little things about him that I never knew was important.

For instance, I found out that Joseph could repair anything in our home. He was an expert electrician, he could make plants grow, he was an excellent cook and he was an avid fisherman. I really believed he inherited his father's skill at construction and learned farming and making things grow from his uncle. It was nice to have a true handy man around the place. Eventually he became employed as an elementary music teacher to two of the schools in the district and I became employed as a sixth grade teacher. I rejoined my former church and made the decision that it was time for my partying days to be over if I was going to be good wife and mother and I committed myself to the Lord. But I did not tell Joseph of my decision.

As usual, I am pregnant again and the pregnancy was not easy. It appeared that each time the pregnancy got worse. The pregnancy this time I was sick all the time. But on September 18, 1971, I gave birth to a bouncing a baby boy, second son. He allowed me to name this son. I named him Leonard Spencer because Leonard meant bold and brave. Cigars and alcohol went around to his friend. A second son! He was proud. He walked around telling everyone about no one was like his wife. He told his friends that anyone could have a girl because the pattern was right under them but to have a boy, the man had to put a special crook in his back. Then things became "normal " again. Joseph was a person who made friends easily. I on the other hand did not. I had to get to know you before I considered the possibility of friendship. Life went on with his being with his friends which led to more drinking and more partying. He finally obtained employment as a Band Director at one of the High Schools in the district. I continued at church and discovered I liked working with young people. A choir was formed and I was the directress. Eventually I was appointed as our church's district youth director. He seemed to strive again. His love was the band and the students. Then I transferred as Reading Teacher to an elementary school where my mother was principal. The elementary school was a part of the school that both of us went to when we were in eighth grade. The youth and I began traveling to every local, district and national function to sing. I was doing what made me happy and Joseph appeared to be doing what made him happy and he continued hitting the streets and the alcohol.

Kool Joe on a warm day

He tried to be a good husband and father but the streets called and he answered. The more he partied and stayed out the more I dedicated myself to church, our children and the choir. He in turn enlisted in the South Carolina National Guard. In June 1974 I graduated with Master's degree in Education and of course I am pregnant again. This time the pregnancy was very difficult and I was sick most of the pregnancy. We are informed by the doctor that if I get pregnant again it would seriously affect my health. We decided this would be our last child and a tubal ligation was performed. On December 12, 1974 our third son was born. We named him Curtis Elliott, Curtis after my father and Elliott after the uncle that reared him. But by that time Joseph had a secret.

Six years later I'm called into the ministry to preach. Hold up! I didn't count on this! I had always vowed that I would never become a preacher. My dad's preaching was enough. How was Joseph going to accept this? One evening I got up enough nerve to tell him about my call and that I needed his permission to continue as a minister. Culture again.? Yes, our church culture dictated that a woman needed her husband's permission to pursue a career outside of the home. As I waited for his answer, he looked at me for the longest time. Then he said " if God called you, I would never stand in your way". I gave my first sermon in May, 1980.

I would travel after school taking classes. I also started teaching adult school one night per week to earn extra money. This kept me busy and I did not become so frustrated about him not being at home. Eventually, Joseph rose to the rank of sergeant in the National Guard. But, in retrospect, Joseph had lost me as his girl. The girl that partied with him was now someone different. I imagined he was confused and frustrated. How does he fit into this seemingly new family? How does he deal with a wife who is a minister and every time he was home he was being pressured every day to stop drinking and partying and change! Now that I think about I didn't just ask him to change, I nagged him every time he came home and we verbally fought about his changing. I considered myself to be an avid debater. I did not consider it nagging. I had been taught by my father how to debate and I was just showing off my skills. However, I did not realize that this man was not reared in my house. To him he considered it nagging and I did not know when to quit. He was not an arguer instead he would leave and head for the streets again. He would look at me before leaving and say "woman you're crazy. It took me years to discover that my nagging pushed him away. Even when I was told that was what I was doing I did not receive it. I was an only child didn't I have the right to look out and defend for myself? Also, when nagging didn't work I would cry realizing he couldn't stand to see me cry. When I would ask him what did I do wrong because he would not stay at home he would hug me and say it was not me or the children, it was him.

Yet, the children grew and thrived. They entered school and as they grew older they excelled in their studies. When they reached high school each of them joined the band. The eldest and middle sons were band drum majors. Two played the trumpet, their dad's instrument of choice, and the eldest also played the guitar and the middle played the saxophone and the organ. Their dad was especially proud of them. It seemed as though they were following in his footsteps but he was very strict and demanded that they be first in whatever they pursued. I on the other hand was the typical mother who felt that he was too strict on them. After all they were my babies. I didn't see that he loved them just as much as I did. He was strict on everything including what they wore because he felt that he had to be strict because he was raising boys who would become men in an unfriendly world to African American men. To get me out of the picture he took them fishing and hunting. He knew I would not interfere there because I hated the outdoors. The children loved it. He played all kinds of war games with them and warned them if they wanted to come with him again they couldn't tell me. And they never did until they got to be men.

Joseph's Big Catch

The drinking and partying continued and by that time he was carrying a secret. He continued disappearing days and sometimes weeks at a time. When he was home his drinking never interfered with his relationship with his sons. It was his concept that what he was doing in the street had nothing to do with him being the head of his house. Trouble struck again and Joseph became sick and had to be admitted in the hospital. Surgery was required and he later recovered. He lost his job for failure to certify his teaching certificate. No matter what the circumstance he found a way to help us survive. He supplemented our income by joining an apprenticeship program learning to repair automobiles. He finally got certification and was rehired as the band director at that High School again. Joseph was extremely talented at what he did, especially as a band director and teacher.

The Maestro at Work

He did not stop his disappearing however. At his last weekly disappearance, I decided that I had enough. In my mind I decided that he was disappearing because he did not want us. I decided that if he didn't want us, then we'd go in another direction. In my mind I felt if we moved before he returned, he would not know where to find us then it'd be over. After that it would be just the children and I. It never entered my mind how hard it would be raising three boys without a father but I was determined to find a better way.

I began looking for another house. I finally engaged the help of a realtor. She found us a home on the opposite side of town. Now the boys could have their own rooms. No more bunk beds. No more three boys in one room. The only thing that hindered my plan was I was very naive about looking for a home. I didn't realize I needed a down payment and I didn't have any money for the down payment. I am devastated. My mother encouraged me to go home and clean up what I have and keep looking. I did what she suggested and I kept looking. Then I believed the Lord moved on the realtor 's heart. She made a contract where I could pay a portion of the down payment each year until I paid the full amount. I quickly signed the contact and went home to tell the children to pack because we were moving. We were all excited. The week we were to move he returned. I do not know who told him we were moving.

When he found out we were moving he asked no questions but eagerly packed his things, rented us a truck and he moved with us to our new home. No, he never explained where he was and I did not pressure him to tell me, I was just happy he was back home, but he had a secret. The year was 1980. I know you are asking why did I let him come with us. Answer: He was my husband. I loved him and he was the children's father. Plus, I had the belief that if he came with us he would change. And also, I read in the Bible in I Corinthians 7 :14 that the unbelieving husband has been sanctified through his wife... and in I Corinthians 7:13 stated that if a woman has a husband who is not a believer and he is willing to live with her, she must not leave him(INV). Those two scriptures became my mantra and I believe it as I prayed another kind of prayer and that was Lord change me.

Joseph in His Uniform

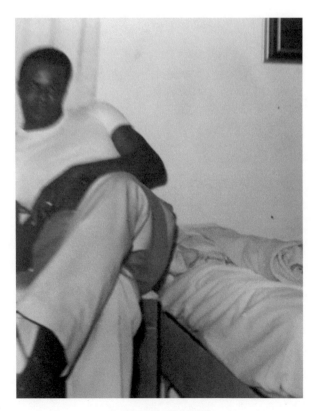

Taking a break

Chapter Six — Life in Our New Home

The children were excited about our new home. No longer do they have to share a room. The house is large enough for us and it appeared that all is right with the world. But, again it seems that the streets and his friends had more influence on him than the boys and I did. However, no matter how loud the streets called, on holidays he was always home, especially Christmas. He made sure that he took the children hunting for a Christmas tree and he got joy out of decorating the Christmas tree. In our forty-nine years together getting the tree and decorating it was his joy. Also, the house was always filled with decorations, presents and food. That was our favorite time of the year. He enjoyed playing Santa Claus and seeing the children opening their presents. He also taught them how to play chess because he believed and taught them that chess was a thinking man's game. And most importantly, chess was where the black pieces had the same equal chance to win as the white pieces. Holiday was over and things became "normal" again.

Again he does not re-certify his teaching certificate and he lost his job again. This time he does not work for six years. To supplement our income, I worked in the summer as a Food Site Coordinator for the district schools. No matter how frustrating it was for all of us, the children succeeded in school, graduated with honors and entered college. The eldest son graduated as an engineer and immediately became employed. By that time, I'm the principal of an elementary school. His partied and staying out did not stop. Every night I would pray Lord change me. I believed that I've got to become a different person if our marriage was going to make it. I also believed if he saw that I have changed surely it would encourage him to change. During that time the middle son entered college. Joseph substituted at the elementary school where I principal. Everyone including the students he taught loved him and he continued in the National Guard.

On Leave

The middle son graduated with a degree in Music and became employed in Florida. Then a friend told me about a rumor she heard and that a young lady was going around saying she had a baby and it was for Joseph. I immediately went home and confronted him and he fervently denied it. Our life continued on its usual course. Two of our children had graduated. In 1994 the uncle that reared him passed away. Our family rallied around him and we got through the processing of grieving. He was not alone. During this time our eldest son entered the ministry. Then tragedy struck. My adopted brother was shot and killed. Joseph rose to the occasion and stood with me during this tragedy always encouraging me that everything would be alright. Then a friend told me again about a rumor she heard and that a young lady was going around saying she had a baby and it was Joseph's. I immediately went home again and confronted him and he fervently denied it. By this time our youngest son has graduated from college. I tried to convince him that if it was true, he needed to admit it and allow the children to grow up together because this was our home and I was not going to leave. He denied that the rumor was true.

Then one evening in 1992 Joseph was late coming home but I'm not disturbed because that was his normal behavior. He later came home and quietly got in bed. The next morning, I saw he was not getting up for work. I asked was he not going to work. He said no, I asked why. He stated because he could not walk. How did you get in bed? I crawled he said. I thought he was not telling the truth and wanted a day off but when I returned he was still in bed. I tried to get him to go to the doctor but he refused. The third day I finally persuaded him to see a doctor. He consented and I took him to the emergency room. Diagnosis: A stroke on the left side of his brain. He stayed in the hospital a week; then rehabilitation. He was permanently disabled on his left side. His career as a band director was over and he retired on disability. His adjustment to retirement was very challenging but soon he attempted to get his life as normal as possible. He cut down on his drinking and staying away from home got fewer. Yet he was keeping a secret.

In 1995 my youngest son graduated from high school and is now in college and tragedy struck again- my father passes away from colon cancer. I'm totally devastated, my encourager and my mentor is gone. The one who called me every Monday morning to inquire about how my Sunday went. He affectionately called me Preacher. But Joseph was there steady as a rock. He never left me and was there for our family. Our lives are like it was in the beginning. After my father's passing Joseph recommitted his life to God and became active in his church again. That year I retired after thirty years in education. Over a period of time he was appointed as the head of the Church 's Administrative Board. During all of our challenges our children grew into matured young men, two of them married and began their families. Joseph and I were so proud that we could participate in their weddings and so pleased to see our grandchildren. Plus, we were getting the privilege of seeing them grow up and enter college. In 1998 we experienced death again, the aunt who reared him passed away. Joseph was totally wiped out. Again he had to deal with those whom he loved leaving him. But, we clung closer together and vowed that we would stay together. In addition, our eldest son entered the ministry.

A Hug and a kiss

Chapter Seven — The Secret Revealed

In 2000, my mother received a telephone call from a young lady. She is trying to locate her father. When questioned concerning who her father was, she stated that her father was Joseph. My mother contacted him and naturally I am informed what's happening. Imagine me finding out that my husband had a daughter he had been hiding for twenty-five years. I immediately confronted him and he finally realizes that he can no longer keep this secret hidden. He confessed and I'm devastated. But, he seemed so relieved that he no longer had to hide this secret.

When the young lady who had an affair with realized that she was pregnant she told him that since she knew he was married before they entered into the relationship she would not cause any trouble she would go away, have the baby and rear their child. He agreed and his life

went on with us. I believed the young lady loved him enough to let him go. She never taught their child to hate her father. Now he does not have to disappear anymore and his children will never accuse him of abandonment. He and I became a family with all of his children. I must admit I was angry with him. Then I began to realize that this was the same man that protected me when I was pregnant with another man's child. This was the same man who protected and looked out for me when I went through my personal struggles. Thinking about it I had to face the fact that I shared some of the blame. I knew he was vulnerable and I became too busy with my personal agenda that I forced him to seek comfort in someone else arms and into sharing his thoughts and dreams with someone else.

Dad always made me laugh

He cried and asked for forgiveness from me and our sons. I forgave him and the children did too. He was my husband again and the children's father. He called his daughter and both of us went to meet her. Overtime, she forgave him. In 2000, she got married and he gave her away.

A few months later I had a heart attack and I had quintuple bypass surgery. He never left my side. I believe my surgery frightened him because he believed that his infidelity had caused my heart attack. From that day until his death he never left me or let me do for him. He always did for me and took care of me. Many times he would tell me that during that time he prayed and asked God if need be take him in my stead. He spent most of his time telling me how he loved me. Also, on quiet evenings as we lay in bed he would say I want to die before you. When I would ask him why he would say he wanted to die before I did because he could not take my dying before he did. I would not know what to do. Then I would say why do you think I could take your going. He would say to me you are stronger than me you could handle it. During that time our middle son is pastor of a church in Alabama and in a few years he is married and father of twins and later he was consecrated as a bishop. We flew to his consecration services. We are proud parents.

In 2003, my first born became ill. Gwendolyn had become a college graduate, employed as church administrator and had an uprising singing career. We called her the Gospel Songbird. After many weeks in the hospital the doctors could not find out what was wrong with her. Finally, they came with the diagnosis: vasculitis, the rare form. All during that time Joseph was the rock for us. In January my beautiful song bird passed away. I was heartbroken. My first born was gone but Joseph was there for all of us. My mother gained a new respect for him. I clung even tighter to him. It appeared that I was losing those who were important to me. It appeared that which I had always feared was becoming a reality. But I still had Joseph.

We became closer. In 2004 I became pastor of my home church. A year later Joseph left his church and joined my church to join me in the ministry. You have to understand this was a huge undertaking for him because he did not have a respect for what they called Holiness. But he believed that the two of us should not be apart anymore. He believed that the two of us should be working together. In his working with our church he experienced the Lord's spirit as he had never before in his local church. He was amazed, yet excited. Finally, he is maturing and I'm getting to first hand see and be a part of his transformation. Life was finally sweet. In 2007, after a church controversy we decided to leave South Carolina and moved to Tuscaloosa, Alabama where our middle son was a pastor. Before we left Joseph had me to understand that he did not really want to go but that he was taking me for my well-being but I had to promise him that if anything happened to him I would bring him back and bury him in South Carolina. I never thought of him dying so I promised. We came to Alabama. We were like two college students again. Hitting the road for another adventure. Just like the college days. Only this time we are two matured human beings that made a decision that both of us agreed on. There would be no stopping us now. As we packed our belongings in our newly built home, both of us knew that this place was our redeeming place. We joined our son's congregation and I became director of Christian Education. Joseph became involved with the youth of the church. His love for teaching was still his pursuit. He taught chess afternoons in one of the public schools. Eventually, he started an instrumental ensemble at the church. His reason was he was tired of seeing the boys play basketball after Life School. He often said that he did not read in the bible that there was ball playing in heaven but he read there was music there. He believed that his gift was teaching and that he was determined to go back to God empty so he started teaching instrumental music at the church. The children loved him and he loved them. The streets may have called him but he no longer had the need to answer. He was at peace because he no longer had to hide secrets. He became an avid gardener and his love of the outdoors returned.

The elder statesman directing

Chapter Eight — The Final Eight Years

After we arrived in Alabama, my youngest son challenged me that I should do something that I had never done before. I told him I wanted to get my doctorate degree. He had me connected with an advisor from Phoenix University online program that day. In 2007 I started to pursue a doctorate degree. My greatest encourager and motivator was my mother who told me every time we talked GO FOR IT. The children were especially proud of me. Joseph was my greatest supporter. He drove me to every residency. I noticed that sometimes he would not get out of bed once we got to residency but I thought he was tired from the drive and just needed to rest. Now as I look back, he was showing signs of his illness and I was so busy with my pursuit I did not see it.

In 2010, I had complication with my heart surgery and entered the hospital. For the first time my mother did not come to visit me and this was strange. But I thought because she was getting up in age she did not want to make the trip from South Carolina to Alabama. After I was discharged, we promised her we would come to see her after I completed what would be my final residency. It was my custom to send my mother flowers on Mother's Day. I sent her flowers and we went to Residency. It was odd for my mother not to call saying she had received the roses. It was so unlike her because she loved roses. I called after each break and received no answer. On Mother's Day I called and still no answer. I finally called a friend to check on her. They found her lying across her bed. My mother was dead. She was eighty-four. I was totally devastated and lost. I felt that everyone I loved was gone. Joseph quickly wrapped his arms around me and said that was not true because he was here. Needless to say, he was my rock. I did not worry during the entire process because I had Joseph. To add to our joy our youngest got married and started a family. Nothing could compare his joy to having his grandchildren around him. Now his life seemed to be complete. We have ten grandchildren.

Then, Joseph experienced a new discovery. Even though he was committed to God and the church, he had never experienced the power of God. He desperately wanted to know the power of God. Then one night at a service, he received the Holy Ghost with the evidence of speaking in tongues. He was afraid yet excited. But that night he knew that what others spoke about was real. We went home that night overwhelmed but happy. Now the two of us had something in common and we could talk about it. I explained to him that the holiness movement began in the Methodist Church of which he was a member all of his life. It was no longer hear say it was real. He was now one of them. The them he had laughed at when he was younger for their dancing and speaking in tongues. We did not know that later he and I would need the Spirit of God to take us through the last leg of our final journey together.

Shortly after my mother's passing, we applied for life insurance and Joseph failed the required examination. His PSA was high. He was referred to a urologist and was diagnosed with prostate cancer. He could not take radiation or chemotherapy. The prognosis required him to take hormonal shots every three months. The side effect was devastating to him. Slowly he was losing what he deemed what made him a man. I tried to encourage him by telling him that part of him did not matter that I loved him and no matter what I would never leave him. His fear and distrust of doctors later led him to refuse further treatments. He kept telling me not to worry that he was going to be alright because God was going to heal him one way or the other. We became very close and depended on each other for support.

In 2014 I went in the hospital. This time it was deemed that I needed two heart stents. The surgeon could only put in one and said it was impossible for him to put in the second. I was not worried because Joseph was there telling me with God I was going to make it and he would never leave me. I began to recognize the change in him. Every morning he would arise at 5:00 am and read his bible and pray. He said he was praying for me, the children and especially his grandchildren. He was especially proud of his grandchildren. He looked forward to seeing the eldest grandchildren graduate from Morehouse and Spellman. He also entertained the idea of being at their wedding. We would often speak about who we thought would be the first grandchild to get married. Then we would shake our heads and laugh. I recovered and in June 2014, I participated in the graduation exercises and received my doctorate in Educational Leadership at the age of 71. To celebrate with me was Joseph and the children. He was so proud of my accomplishment always telling me I was stronger than I knew or believed. Joseph was my motivator and my severest critic. Many times he would say to me "I'm glad you stayed with me because if you hadn't I would have been dead long ago." Sometimes he would sometimes just call to me and say "come here I need a hug". No matter what either one of us was doing we'd stop and hug each other tight. Then he would lean back and smile and sometimes he would sing to me "If I had a nickel, I'd spend it all on candy and give it all to you, cause baby I love you." I would say to him Well baby, it is what it is. I love you regardless. He would say no, I love you more than you know. His singing would make me laugh because he couldn't carry a tune.

Receiving my Doctorate

In 2015, I was placed in the hospital to receive the second heart stent. The surgeon deemed upon examination that he could not put in another stent because my heart bypass grafts were closing. Immediately we began looking for another doctor. Our youngest son found us a doctor in Atlanta. At the same time a doctor was found for Joseph. Upon examination they found his PSA had risen. He was referred to a urologist. The immediately resumed his treatment. A CAT scan showed that the cancer had invaded his bones. But the doctors did not seem concerned. He felt that if the cancer could be contained in the bones, Joseph had a fighting chance. In my wildest dreams, it never entered my mind that I would lose Joseph to this beast called prostate cancer.

We would make our trips to the doctors and we came back home feeling encouraged. Our special time was shopping in thrift and antique shops and eating at O'Charley's and the Fish Market in Marietta. Our fun time was at night when it was bedtime. He loved it when I did not stay up after he retired. He loved it when I would go to bed with him. When I would get in bed he would open his arms and I would lay in the crook of his arms and place my head on his chest listening to his heart beat. He would hold me until I fell asleep. This was our ritual for eight years. It was like it was in the beginning, always experiencing and enjoying being in each other's presence. This made up for all the nights that he had spent away from me. Many times he would say "don't worry girl I'm here." He called me girl when he was pleased with me and woman when he was upset with me.

Enjoying lunch at one of our favorite spots

He was especially excited when it was time for the Impact Instrumental Ensemble to perform. His latest plans for them was to perform at the church's African American History Moments. They were planning on performing "Dem Bones', a piece he had played when he was in the band at college. On October 28, we kept our appointment to the doctor. At that time, he received a flu shot. A few days later he said he felt like he was getting a cold. Then a few days later he complained that he could not lie down because he was in pain. A week past by and the pain continued. I got in touch with the urologist and he prescribed something for pain.

On October 31st I noticed that he did not have an appetite and he did not want anything to drink but he insisted that we get dress and attend the Impact Silver Ball. The church was celebrating its 25th Church Anniversary. At the ball when the music started he grabbed my hand just like he grabbed it in college and said let's dance. We went on the floor and he held me tight and we waltzed to the music even though the music was fast. We were not in step but we did not care. I felt like we were the only people in the room and I was his queen.. Little did I know that that would be our last dance together.

The Last Dance

His birthday came, November 5 th and we celebrated his 73rd birthday. A few weeks he was still complaining of pain. I tried to encourage him to get in touch with the doctor. He would say no it will be better tomorrow. I knew that he was afraid of doctors and shots. He would not go if he could avoid it. As the weeks progressed he got worse. I noticed that he would move from the bed to his chair and would not go outside. This was unusual for him because he loved being outdoors and gardening. His final confederate rose that he was working on for a long time bloomed. Instead of going outside to see the plant, he instructed our son to open the blinds and let him see it and asked him to take a picture. Then one evening upon attempting to get out of his chair, we found he could not walk. I still could not persuade him to go to the doctor. Joseph was a man who believed he had control of himself and whatever situation he encountered. He never liked the idea that someone had control of what he thought, said or felt.

His Last Confederate Rose

Finally, I called our son. He came and he and my daughter-in-law persuaded him to go the emergency room. He was admitted to the hospital. During his stay the doctors had a CAT scan performed. There they found that the cancer had gone to his liver. They worked on his dehydration and he began to feel a little better. He kept saying that he wanted to go home. A couple of days before Thanksgiving the doctors released him with the understanding that he would consult his doctors in Atlanta. The children and their families came for Thanksgiving but Joseph still could not walk and he was still always in pain. After Thanksgiving, my eldest and youngest sons and I went to Atlanta. His primary physician had arranged that he be admitted to the hospital there.

And still I never entertained the idea that he would not make it. After many examinations, cancer specialists were consulted and came to give their final prognosis. They informed us that the cancer had metastasized in the liver and Joseph had two to three weeks to live. In my mind this still did not register because he told me he would never leave me. We still could not get him to eat, but he kept telling me not to worry everything was going to be alright. All he wanted me to do was to hold his hand. I spent my birthday, November 29, 2015 in the hospital with Joseph. The doctors estimated that he had two to three weeks to live. I still refused to believe that Joseph was going to die. We started making plans for him to be transferred to hospice.

The night of December 3, I played the music he loved and played the audio bible of the twenty-third psalms. He repeated each word and then he said to me "that's enough now, let's go to sleep. We went to sleep and the next morning around eight I awoke to Joseph making a strange noise, I arose and asked him was he in pain. He did not answer but I kept hearing the noise. Then I rang for the nurse. They came in and tried to rouse him but he did not respond. After taking him for another CAT scan, they returned and informed me that Joseph had gotten worse and that his ride to hospice would prove fatal. They asked me what I wanted them to do. I replied "Make him better, I'm not ready for this". One of the physicians said "you might not be ready, but this is going to happen." He apologized later for his harshness. Then I calmed down and asked to go back in the room with Joseph. By that time, I had called the children and they were on the way to the hospital. I also called his brother who came to visit him and he also came over. My youngest son arrived and we gathered around his bed and spoke to him reassuring him that we were there and that they would take care of me and we played his favorite music. At 12:00 pm on December 4, 2015 Joseph calmly passed away. My world and all I knew about living was gone. Yes, the Renaissance Man took his flight to Omega Chapter on Alpha Phi Alpha's Founders Day, the fraternity he loved. He never did anything normal. He was always calm and as in the past he did not panic. His funeral service was held December 12, on his youngest son's birthday. He never did anything ordinary. **And of course, All of his children and I took him back to South Carolina for his burial. A promise kept.**

Our children

Epilogue

Many who read this story will ask the question why did I stay with him. Most of his life he put up barriers to hide how he truly felt. You must understand that we grew up in an era where men were taught not to let your woman see your struggle or let them see your weaknesses. You were told to always suck it up. It did not matter to me because I love him then and now more than I ever did. My journey with him needs no explanation. We were two imperfect people who lived our lives together. We learned how to forgive each other while loving each other hard and we were determined that both of us had the best of all worlds. To me he was the most exciting part of my life. He always found a way to make me excited when he was in the room and I believed I did the same for him. We realized that neither one of us could have walked out and never return but both of us realize we were destined to be together. Each of us lived out the creed and our covenant that we made as a young couple in 1966 that whom God joined together let no man put asunder. I refused to take the advice of some and jump ship because I knew that some of them that were giving me the advice would jump in my ship with him as soon as I left. In addition, we believed the rest of the covenant that said that in sickness and in health we belonged together. Our journey showed what true forgiveness and love will do. My life will never be the same. I am still in the grieving process and I expect if I live twenty more years I will still be missing him. Through all our challenging experiences I never felt that he did not love me but I finally understood that he was struggling with coping with losing those he loved and with knowing and accepting who he was. I too now must continue to struggle with the beast of loneliness and my fear of being alone. My head knows that Joseph is in a better place but my heart still yearns for him to be with me. With God's continued help I vow to beat this demon that torment me and not only me but so many who are reading my story. Also, I must continue to struggle with what I have feared all my life the fear of being left alone. My constant solace is that I have come to realize that I am not alone. I feel the presence of God and the presence of Joseph every day. Sometimes it makes me smile and sometimes it makes me cry. But my crying is not in dismay. I cry in hope that one day I will be reunited with him again. Not on this earth but in a higher plain of existence.

When I attempted to tell some of my children and others his life story. The Spirit of the Lord revealed to me that I did not understand him. It was further revealed that in order to really tell another man's story one must understand his journey. Joseph's journey included the experience of the loss of his mother at age eight and also at the same time experienced abandonment by his father. All of his life he struggled with distrust of those who loved him. He was always waiting for the one he loved to leave him. My struggle was that because I was an only child, I would someday be left alone. So I clung to him more tightly as I lost those I loved. You see, without realizing it both of us had the same issues. We just could not know how to communicate to each other about our real fears and struggles. I believe Joseph always knew what I feared and he tried all he could to make me feel safe. For the last two months, I would wake up crying every morning. This pain inside of me just won't let me rest. One morning I woke up and the spirit of the Most High spoke to me and said "You think I've done you wrong, don't you? Of course I did not answer. I just listened. Then the Spirit said "I let you know him for sixty years and also I let you be married to him for forty-nine years. I could have taken him anytime especially when he was running the streets and having a good time. But if I had done that you would not have seen how I can transform a diamond in the rough. I allowed him to fulfill his purpose on earth. I got him ready so that you will be able to see him again". Then I could have taken you, it would not have been a surprise to anyone. But if I had taken you first it would have totally destroyed him and he would have lost faith in me. He left having faith in you and the God both of you served.

Then I dried my eyes and dressed. I will not say I don't cry because I really miss him every second, every minute, every hour of the day. But I can imagine when I meet him again he will say to me "Girl I've been waiting on you. What took you so long". Then he will open his arms and smile and say, "I NEED A HUG". Then he'll lean back and smile and say I love you girl." Then he'll grab my hand and we'll walk around Heaven. Then we will finally be together again.

I need another hug

Final Lessons learned:

1. Take time to listen to your body and always take time to take care of yourself.

2. Forgive quickly and always love hard.

3. Learn to communicate effectively. Always find time to tell your mate what is on your mind or what is troubling you.

4. Support the dreams and goals of your partner.

5. Speak the truth in love.

6. Don't romanticize your mate shortcomings. Accept them and always pray that the Lord allow you to see yourself.

7. Don't' be a Nagger. Proverbs 21:9 states "Better to live on the corner of the roof than to share a house with a nagging wife. (NIV)

Kool Joe resting easy

Printed in the United States
By Bookmasters